Talking with Tebé

Clementine Hunter, Memory Artist

Talking with Tebé

Clementine Hunter, Memory Artist

Edited by Mary E. Lyons

Houghton Mifflin Company

Boston 1998

To Rufus and Emma

The text of this book is set in Aries.
Book design by Lisa Diercks

Library of Congress Cataloging-in-Publication Data
Hunter, Clementine.
    Talking with Tebé : Clementine Hunter, memory artist / edited by Mary Lyons.
        p.   cm.
    Includes bibliographical references.
    ISBN 0-395-72031-1
    1. Hunter, Clementine. 2. Afro-American painters — Louisiana — Natchitoches —
Biography. I. Lyons, Mary E. II. Title.
    ND237.H915A2 1998
    759.13—dc21
    [B]   97-42253
                                                                            CIP
                                                                            AC

Printed in Singapore
TWP 10 9 8 7 6 5 4 3 2 1

Contents

Editor's Note

When I was a child in South Carolina, I learned an important lesson about field labor. One bright fall day, my fourth-grade class went on a field trip. It truly was a trip to a field—a cotton field. For thirty minutes, we children stooped over to pluck cotton bolls from their scratchy black casings.

The landowner gave each of us a dime for our labor and invited us into his nearby country store. Picking cotton was hot, thirsty work. With my money, I bought a bottle of "Co-Cola," as we say in the South.

At the time it seemed like great fun, but years later I understood the real lesson of that trip. If the landowner had paid a nickel for each drink (a likely price in 1956), he had doubled his money, and I had empty pockets.

The Melrose Plantation store in Clementine Hunter's time was near the fields, too. Workers were paid each week in money or paper scrip. They traded scrip at the store for flour, sugar, beans, salt, and meat.

At first this wage-labor system seems fair. Workers could exchange labor for food and were offered rent-free cabins. "I believe I have lived in every cabin on Melrose," Clementine Hunter once said of the Louisiana plantation where she worked for over seventy-five years.

But the plantation controlled the wages and the price of food. As a low-paid field worker and servant, Hunter could never earn enough to buy a cabin for herself. Yet her labor helped make Melrose the largest privately owned pecan plantation in the world. Clementine Hunter's art, then, is more than an amusing picture of the past. It is a valuable record of how plantation owners became richer as workers stayed poor.

One book and more than eighty articles have been written about Clementine Hunter. Some writers have called her a creative genius. To others, especially those before the 1970s, she was not a real artist but a "plantation Negro." Many were surprised that an older woman with no training could produce art at all.

These notions convinced me that it was time Hunter spoke for herself. Most of the text in *Talking with Tebé* is written in her own words. I gathered quotations from magazines, newspapers, and twenty-two taped interviews made by Hunter's friend, Mildred Bailey, in 1978. A few quotations are from newspaper columns by François Mignon, the curator of Melrose.

To tell Clementine Hunter's story, I put events in order and combined her thoughts on a particular subject. For clarity, I inserted dates and place names. When her words were confusing to read, I changed a word, phrase, or sentence to ease the transition from speech to written text.

Hearing Hunter's rich Creole accent on tape was as satisfying as eating a piece of pecan pie. I felt as if I were sitting in the same room with her and her dog, Tiny. Though her voice had grown deep and hoarse with age, it was strong and confident. When she laughed, I laughed with her. When she spoke softly, I sensed a reluctance to discuss some topics.

For example, the artist had little to say about the Association for the Preservation of Historic Natchitoches. In 1977 the association became the new owner of Melrose. It raised $7,000 by selling her posters at a party held for her hundredth birthday. The money was used to modernize her old cabin, paint it white, and move it closer to Melrose's big house.

Hunter's former studio now sits prettily behind the big house. But one local person noted that the building "never looked that nice when Clementine lived there." It puzzles me that Hunter had to worry about payments on her new mobile home while her art financed an empty exhibit cabin.

Perhaps she was afraid to complain about the unfair use of funds. Yet she was refreshingly outspoken on other subjects. As one of her acquaintances said, "Clementine didn't say a whole lot, but when she did, you better be listening!"

So I listened carefully when she spoke of her former employer, Sister Cammie Henry. Cammie was famously difficult. Her son recalls that she was an alcoholic whose moods "ran hot and cold." And François Mignon remembered that Clementine Hunter "did not always have a pleasant time cooking for the Henry family. The personality of some of the members jarred her nerves." After Hunter became well known, Cammie was friendlier. She telephoned often, visited Hunter at her mobile home, and even asked her to live with her. Clementine Hunter was unimpressed by the attention. Though she was not well traveled in the world, she was wise to its ways.

"Seem to me I can set Cammie straight when she comes here," Hunter said forcefully on one of the tapes. "I can fix her up good!" A remark, it seems to me, that was pure-dee Clementine.

Pronunciation Key

Bubba's: Buh-BUH's

branle: Brawh

Clémence: Clee-MAWH

Clementiam: Clee-MEN-shum

Coin Coin: QUAN-quan

Creole: CREE-ole

Dupré: DU-pree

Ewe: E-vay

François Mignon: frahn-SWA meen-YŌN

Ibo: E-bo

Isle Brevelle: IH-bruh-vil

Mé-Mé: MAY-may

Natchitoches: NACK-uh-tish

Petit Bébé: puh-TEE Bay-BAY

Tebé: TEE-bay

Meet Tebé

Tebé was a stylish dresser who liked to wear jewelry and a wig.

Clementine Hunter lived her long life in the Cane River region of northwest Louisiana. The Cane forms the eastern boundary of a thirty-mile strip of land called Isle Brevelle. The river's slow-moving current is dark, and on a sunny day it glistens like molasses.

Double-winged dragonflies skim by, their wings doubled again in the watery mirror. Wild carrot lines the banks with lacy blooms. Here and there a dead cypress tree pokes through the surface and raises skeletal arms to the sky. The Cane is a river of mystery. *Follow me*, it seems to say. *I have a story to tell.*

Clementine Hunter, called Tebé by her family, was born at the southern end of the river in 1886. The Emancipation Proclamation had ended slavery in 1863, so Tebé was not born enslaved. But as a manual laborer, she lived a slavelike existence.

For decades after the war, many former slaves and their descendants worked for wages on plantations. They lived in shabby cabins that belonged to the landowners. Both men and women toiled all week in the hot sun of the fields, and on Saturday the landowner would tally their pay. Sometimes he cheated them by using a "crooked pencil" to subtract money owed for rent and food. This could leave workers with no funds or even in debt to the landowner.

Tebé's art tells the laborers' story. In colors as bright as a Louisiana sky, she shows

"Gathering the Figs," circa 1950
Tebé "squeezed" time in her paintings, so that everything happens at once.

the backbreaking work required to pick cotton, gather figs, cut sugar cane, and harvest pecans. Tebé knew that women did the jobs of both men and women, whether in the heat of a kitchen or the heat of a field. She often highlighted female workers by making them the largest figures.

Tebé's art portrays good times, too. Scenes of baptisms, weddings, and church socials celebrate a rich community life that helped the workers survive. These are paintings of rest and play, of joy and hope.

To tour Tebé's world, throw away your clock. In her day, workers told time by watching the sun march across the sky. You won't need a calendar, either. When spring arrived, it was time to plow the fields. In summer, people hoed the cotton that they picked in the fall. They knew winter was coming on when pecans began to drop from the trees.

The workers traveled on foot or in a mule-drawn cart. The phrases "just up the road a piece" and "way over yonder" were all they needed to measure a mile.

Every language has two sides, formal and informal. Tebé's voice in the following memoir is relaxed and informal. For example, she says, "The children was joining together" instead of "The children joined together."

Speakers of West African languages use similar grammar. In the Ibo language, there is no difference between singular and plural nouns. In the Ewe language, *go, went,* and *going* are the same word, so that past events seem to be happening now.

Like her African ancestors, Tebé invites us to enter her story in the present tense. "When I sits, I sits loose," she once said. Sit loose and enjoy your talk with her. Let the artist's lively words and colorful pictures carry you way down yonder to Cane River as it was one hundred years ago.

Girlhood

"Card Playing," circa 1978. The oversized cards show that playing poker was one of Tebé's favorite pastimes.

I don't pay much attention to time. It doesn't bother me and I don't bother it. It's all in the way you think about it, anyhow. Folks say one thing about age, I say another. Time is nothing but a play-pretty—a hawk on wheels.

Here on Isle Brevelle, time runs deep as the Cane River. I love it back here on the river. This is my native, and I'm used to it. I sleep a few hours, then lie there thinking about pictures. I get up and mark out a picture and then I paint it.

I don't pass for knowing about painting. Other folks say they get training and paint by rules. I can't paint my pictures by rule. I paint them by heart.

Paintings catch memories a-crossing my mind. Pictures of the hard part of living. The easy parts, too, like fishing and dancing, playing cards and blind man's bluff, Easter and Christmas.

You know the Christmas story from the Bible? That's Mary and the baby Jesus and the angels and the three wise men taking him a present. One of them got a cake, and one got a gourd, and one got a present in a box. It just be candy.

The house—I call it the little red house—is the baby's house. He was born there. See the angels flying up in the air? That their hair flying up like that. If you flew through the air, your hair would do that, too.

I was born around Christmas 1886 at Marco's Plantation. Way down yonder at the end of the road. *Way* down yonder . . . you don't see no birds, you don't see nothing down where I was born. Three months later, on March 19, 1887, I was baptized in St.

"Nativity Scene," circa 1970
Streaked winter clouds display Tebé's fine sense of color.

John's Catholic Church in Cloutierville. Cloochyville, we call it. Up the road a piece from Marco's.

My baptism name is Clementiam, but I got other names. Clémence, now that's my sure-enough name. It's French, you see. I'm little, so my family called me Petit Bébé or Bébé. Sometimes just Tebé. I'm five feet tall and weigh ninety-eight pounds. I don't eat much.

I ain't ever traveled much myself. All my life I lived right around Cane River, more or less. Mostly I have lived at Melrose Plantation, what's owned by Mrs. Cammie Henry.

The big house on Melrose. The family of Marie Coin Coin, a former slave, founded the plantation around 1796.

I came up to Melrose when I was not a little girl and not old enough to marry. I never did go back to Marco's.

I was an older girl when I changed my name to Clementine. It's more easy to say. I put that *tine* in there. Just changed it myself. Rhymes with *mean*. Like Sister Benedict that was my teacher at school in Cloochyville. Sister Benedict—you know her? She was *mean!*

I went there for one year, and I learned a few letters of the ABCs. But I wasn't much for school. The big girls used to tease us smaller girls and poke at us with sticks. I wasn't having any of that. I got me a stick and poked back!

I quit when I just would fight all the time. You see, the white children and the colored children was joining together. They had a fence between us, you know, our school on this side, the white school on that side.

One time I tell Sister Benedict, I say, "Sister, can I go and get some water?" and she say, "Yeah, go ahead and hurry back and get to your lesson." And before she know one thing, I had done gone to the cistern to get water and jumped the fence and gone home.

Another time Sister Benedict checked my bucket and found some meat. Back then, Catholics weren't allowed to eat meat on Friday, but I was going to eat it unbeknownst to her. I told her it wasn't mine, but she threw my bucket away. I ran to the road. Sat down until the school out. The other children told my mother. She whipped me and sent me back the next day, but it didn't do no good. Go back again, run off again. Never did learn nothing.

"Graduation," circa 1950
Tebé received an honorary doctorate in fine arts from Northwestern State Louisiana University in 1986.

I told Mama, "I'd rather go pick cotton." In those days picking cotton was easy to me. You *know* I was crazy! But I was needed at home. Papa and Mama and my three brothers and three sisters all worked. We had to scuffle to keep things going.

My People

We are Creole people, a mix-up people. Got more different kinds of blood than any other people. All the folks here on lower Cane River are Creoles—speak nothing but Creole French.

My mama's name was Mary Antoinette Adams. Her mama, Idoles, was a slave. That's a funny name, an old-time name. Idoles didn't come from around here in Louisiana. She was brought from a place called Old Virginia, back before the Civil War. She lived to be 110! Her husband, Billy Zack Reuben, was from Virginia and a slave, too. He fell in Cloochyville and broke his neck. That's how he died.

Rare nineteenth-century photographs of Tebé's father, Janvier Reuben, and her mother, Antoinette Adams Reuben

"Wake," circa 1943
Candles, flowers, and mourners seem to float on top of one another. Self-taught painters often stack images in their art.

My daddy's daddy? Well, you know them horse traders? Maybe you ain't seen them, but you heard talk of them. Traders used to pass through here in the olden times. My grandfather was an Irishman who traded horses up and down the road during the war.

He traveled everywhere. I guess he had seen everything, too. He just got tired of it all. He said he'd had enough of this world. He went into the chicken house and cut his throat. His wife found him there. The razor was yet in his hand.

"Arc en Ciel—Angels and Rainbow," 1979
"The white angels are going to heaven," Tebé said. "The red ones are going to hell."

Grandmother was a black Indian woman. We called her Mé-Mé. She was a little low woman with long hair. I know her good! She was never sick. Never had any ailments. If she sometimes felt poorly, she made up some different kinds of brew from roots of plants and trees. This made her well.

She went barefoot till the day she died. She mashed her toe one day and it gave her a poison of some kind. She had saved all her clothes and put them in a trunk and locked them up. When she died, they had her clothes to bury with her. Put them in the coffin. They used to do that, you know.

When somebody dies here on Cane River, they wake the body right at the church. Watch it all night, say prayers. Next day they pull the coffin to the grave in a mule cart. Put the coffin in a hole in the ground and ring the church bell.

People just a-dying. They sure going away fast, I can tell you that. A burying most every day. But you going when your time come. Long as it don't come, you ain't going! When I die, I hope I will be an angel. I'm going to try hard to be one. Try hard.

Field Work

"Cotton Picking," early 1970s. "Goosters" are eating bugs between rows of cotton. According to Tebé, a gooster was a rooster mixed with a goose.

When I was young, everything on the farm was cotton crops. My daddy used to work until it look like he generally had no sense. He'd get in the middle of two rows and pick on each row at the same time. Pick four hundred pounds of cotton in a day.

Or plowing . . . Some mornings the men went to the mule lots so early you couldn't see the mules. Thing to do was to feel around until you had your own mule for the day.

I work hard in my days, too. I was about fifteen or sixteen when I pick cotton. The young ones pick cotton, and the old ones pick cotton, all of them.

You hang the sack over your shoulder. Pull the sack until it get heavy. When it get heavy, pull it to the end of the row and they weigh it. That'd be a hundred pounds, no less than fifty. They write it down and pay you when Saturday come. Pick some more, empty that. Then you put the cotton in a basket and put it up in the cotton house.

I was picking in fields on the back of our house at Melrose. Wore a dress. I never did wear no pantses like they do now. I wear a hat. Put it on my head sometimes. Sometimes I wouldn't. We like to lay back there in that cotton. Wouldn't sleep but you could get up in there and rest.

I couldn't pick no dew cotton. In the morning, early, that cotton full of dew. It wasn't too heavy, it just stick on my hands. I wait until the dew dry, about ten o'clock, then I pick cotton. I was done about five o'clock, I reckon. The sun was way up yonder then.

"Pecan Threshing," circa 1975
Workers flail branches with bamboo sticks to make the pecans fall.

Cotton picking could last right on through the New Year. And during this cotton-picking time there was also pecan picking.

I always liked to pick pecans. It was hard work. You had to stoop over a lot. You had to gather at least three hundred pounds or better a day to make it worthwhile. Extra money was made by pecan picking. Life was hard, but if you toughed it out you could get by. During the times when money was scarce and they wasn't too much to eat, a pinch of snuff helped kill the appetite.

"Fishing on Cane River," 1975
Tebé enjoyed fishing with her grandson, who carried the bucket while she carried the pole.

After working all week, Saturday night was a big night. They had a juke place across the river by Saint Augustine's Church, but the people would mostly make whiskey in their house. They'd cook their whiskey at home so the law couldn't catch them.

People had a better time than now. Sometimes we'd dance all night. Or fish. Catch the catfishes and breams with earthworms. Stay on the bank—I don't get in no boat. Then we have a fish fry.

"Zinnias Looking at You!," early 1960s
Tebé usually painted zinnias on a dark background.

Or we picked flowers and hauled them home in a cart. God makes flowers grow everywhere, and these he makes grow in my mind. See those zinnias in the picture? They my favorite 'cause they looking straight out at you!

Marriage and Children

Mama died at Melrose in 1905. Died with the dropsy.
I ain't cried when my mama died. You know, when you don't cry when
your mother dies, well, you ain't going to cry. It hurt me, but I just can't
cry. Can't do that, and that's why I don't go to funerals now.

"Funeral," circa 1955. Creole people regard it as an honor to carry flowers at a funeral.

"Couple Dancing," circa 1980
A couple dances to rhythm and blues music at Bubba's, a bar near Melrose Plantation.

My daddy? Well, my daddy just got sick. You know how old folks is. Running around when they try to make theirself young. My daddy wasn't no old man, but he had a good age. And he used to run around too much, and he got sick, and the doctor couldn't do nothing.

At sixteen or so, I was keeping company with Charlie Dupré. Cuckoo Charlie, they called him. He was smart—built a piano and a steam engine when he'd never seen either one. Our boy Frenchie was born in 1907. Then Cora came. Charlie died around 1914.

After Charlie died, I met Emmanuel Hunter, a wood chopper for the Henry family. Met him at a dance on Melrose. A good dance—a Saturday night dance. Later, at another dance, he asked me to marry him. We married in January 1924, and we lived in a cabin back of Melrose.

In the wedding picture, the groom, he is kind of important, but he don't count much 'longside the bride. The mother of the bride is in charge of the wedding cake, the size of which shows if the wedding is any account. And the preacher is a little low man. Sometimes trouble is already starting. See how mean the bride is looking and how the groom is staring at the ceiling?

I was scared when I got married. I said, "I don't know that man!" I had a good husband, though. Emmanuel and I started off all right and stayed together for a good many years. We didn't have too much fuss. I think marriage is good for people if they are suited to each other.

"Wedding," circa 1955
When Tebé's paint supply ran low, she thinned what she had with turpentine.

I spoke French until I married Emmanuel. He taught me to speak American. Some of his people used to teach school at night at Melrose. Oh well, I went to night school, but I was just running in the moonlight. I didn't learn nothing. And I have made out all right, too.

All my life I have had a strong mother wit, which is better than stuff you learn from books. A heap of folks got book learning running out of their ears, but I can't say they is smart people.

Emmanuel and I had three children, King, Mary, and Agnes. I gave birth to seven children in all, just like my mama. Two born dead—I didn't name them 'cause they weren't baptized. My living ones, they call me Mama Tebé.

I didn't have no baby-sitters like they do now. Mine sat in the field at the end of the cotton row. Sometime I'd find some of them fast asleep in the weeds.

Pick cotton—one hundred and fifty pounds, sometimes two hundred, I pick. All that was fifty cents a hundred, that's all they was getting. Fifty cents a hundred and I done dragged my children all in the field.

Or I put them in a tree in a branle. A branle was a kind of swing hung to a tree limb with a rope. Us mamas could go up and down a cotton row and still keep an eye on the baby in the branle. And the baby could swing back and forth that way all day. The mama could take time out now and then to feed the child.

One day a friend of mine, Ethel, had her baby in a branle. We looked back once and the whole thing was on fire. The branle and the baby both burned up. What happened was a bird picked up a

"Baptism," circa 1943
Tebé liked to paint baptisms best. "I saw them people go in the water a-many, a-many, a-many a time," she once said.

lighted cigarette and dropped it right on that cradle. Wasn't nothing anybody could have done about it.

My children, I raise them all—had a time. I no paint that. Had them baptized in the Catholic church, but all my grandchildren were baptized in the Baptist church. In the picture, they is baptizing down there in the lake. Not in front of the church—further from the church, other side of the bridge. That's the little children they gonna baptize.

Housework

I washed out many a line of clothes in my day for Cammie Henry's family and my own. Times without number I spent at the washpots on Melrose Plantation. Sometimes I get a misery in my back. Many a time you get everything washed and hung out to dry and the clothesline breaks, and there it is all to do over again.

Mama taught me to cook. I make gumbo, pecan pies, cornbread, boiled crawfish. You can eat crawfish with rice, or you can stuff them and all like that.

After I got married, I left the field and come to cook for Cammie Henry. She didn't like no fancy stuff. She like all old-time cooking. I used to walk back and forth from my house to her big house. Across the river spillway. It's a good little walk.

I didn't cook regular, just sometime I'd help out. Most of the cooking were for Cammie's five children. Wasn't all that much strain, just on the holidays. They good children,

"Wash Day," n.d.
To scrub clothes by hand, women hauled water from the river in buckets. Then they chopped firewood to heat the water.

except for her daughter, Cammie Junior. The one they call Sister. She *mean!*

Mrs. Cammie Henry had a lot of company—writers, painters. People coming and going, all of them in a stir-up. They come to Melrose to paint and write, but they didn't live there. I brought ice for their drinks, and many's the pot of coffee I set down for them. They joked I'd be serving coffee when they got to heaven.

"Cooking in the Yard," n.d.
François Mignon published Tebé's favorite recipes in
the Melrose Plantation Cookbook.

I cooked for them people, too. Game soup, boiled bass, barbecued ham, parsnip fritters, apple biscuits, brown bread, fig cake, puddings . . . "Here is Louisiana cooking at its best!" they said.

Mama taught me to sew. I used to sew a lot. I made many a quilt cover in my day. Make them on paper or corn sacks so they'd be stiff. Nobody a-tall gave me the idea. I just start to fooling with them, that's all. Somebody give me some scraps.

Well, you see, I cut the size of sack I wanted and put the pieces on it. But you got to know how to put the pieces together. I had to learn that—how to put them together. Pretty easy after that. And they *heavy*! They too heavy to hang on the wall. They was good for a heavy cover. Make them to put on the bed, like a person's going on a long trip in the wintertime.

Made dolls, too. Making dolls was easy. Get me an empty wine bottle, pad the neck with cotton and cloth sewed around to make the bust part, make a head out of cotton and a sock, the arms out of wire and cloth, and put on a little hat. Looked pretty good.

Painting

I liked needlework, sketching, just doing anything with my hands. Then in the 1930s Alberta Kinsey came here from New Orleans to paint magnolias, and I had to clean up her room. She gave me some old tubes of paint to throw in the trash, but I didn't pay her no mind. I kept them and tried marking up some pictures in my cabin. Nobody taught me to mark them. I did it myself 'cause I knew how to do that.

My first picture I painted on a shoebox top. I didn't have no board like I got now. I didn't show the painting to anybody. I thought I'd give it away. Didn't think it wasn't worth nothing to keep.

I never watched Alberta paint. I was busy cooking—didn't have time! Except once when she was stumped on a painting of a cotton field. Alberta said, "I can't figure this out. What in the world am I going to do?"

And Mrs. Cammie Henry said, "Well, why don't you ask Clementine? She can always solve all problems. Take her with you to the studio."

Tebé's four-by-sixteen-foot murals line the inside walls of the African House.

The studio was out back in the African House, a brick-and-cypress house them slaves built a long time ago. So I went out there and pointed to a spot on Alberta's canvas and said, "If it was me, I'd put one of them bales of cotton right there."

Half-hour later, Alberta said the whole idea for the picture came together. Just unrolled in her head after my visit. But I paint whatever comes in my mind. Whatever hits me. People say they likes my pictures. Me, I don't know, I just paints them.

No matter how tired I is when it comes night, as soon as I light that oil lamp, a whole lot of things start going across my brain, and before I knows it, I am getting them things down on paper. Sometimes the lines don't go right and I have to spoil them out with an eraser.

I used to keep Emmanuel up at night with my painting "Woman," he said one time, "if you don't stop painting and get some sleep, you'll go crazy."

"No," I said, "if I don't get this painting out of my head, I'll sure go crazy."

"Plastic Milk Jug," mid-1970s
Tebé also painted on snuff jars, wine bottles, cast-iron kettles, and frying pans.

I was still cooking at Melrose when François Mignon came in September 1938. So blind, he almost couldn't see nothing when he come here. I'm the one showed him around in that yard.

François was a writer. He stayed on at Melrose, and we got to be friends. One time he gave me a window shade to paint on. The one hanging in his room in the Ghana House. That's an outbuilding on Melrose. He hated that shade. It flapped all the time in the wind, you see. Five o'clock next morning, I tapped on his door and showed him my painting of a baptism.

"Sister, you don't know it," he said, "but this is just the first of a whole lot of pictures you are going to bring me in the years ahead."

So I went to painting. I painted every time I wasn't doing nothing. I took up anything I could paint on. Sometimes if I was going down the road and saw a board what

*Tebé in 1950, when she was about sixty-four. "That's
pure me!" she said when she saw her photograph once.*

I could paint on, I'd pick it up and paint on that. Once I took my own window shade down and painted on it.

Alberta, she didn't bring me no new paint that she bought, but she'd leave me the paint what she painted with. Or Mrs. Henry would paint with the children, and she would give me that paint. It was good paint.

François bought me some paints from Sears and Roebuck, and he showed my pictures to Mr. Pipes. Mr. Pipes was a writer that came to Melrose back in 1943. He liked my pictures, too. After he left, he sent paint and boards to François, then François give them to me.

Mr. Pipes told some people I was an artist, and they gave me money so I could keep painting. One time Mr. Pipes sent me money himself. I don't like to borrow, and if I borrow I know I got to pay and it just worry me, you know. I been like that. But one winter Mr. Pipes sure done kept us'es from freezing and I thank him in the most high.

That was the winter Emmanuel took sick. Wasn't anybody but me to pay the doctor's bills and buy clothes for my grandchildren. Some people passed by the cabin and wanted my pictures. They wouldn't go away unless I would sell to them. So François made me a sign that said "Art Exhibit. Admission 25¢. Thanks."

But I worried I was cheating people, 'cause when the Lord give the gift of painting to me, He didn't say rich, and He didn't say sell. He just give it to me.

So if folks come here looking for an artist, I tell them I ain't no artist, I'm a painter. I sets things down in paint and that is all there is to it, but I sure ain't no artist. Like

Tebé often wore a head wrap, a dress custom from Africa.

chickens—I find chickens the hardest things to paint. I just can't no ways paint a chicken.

After Emmanuel died, in 1944, I moved to another cabin on Melrose. The last house on Shoo Shoo Lane, the one near my son King. Kept on painting while I was still working in the big house. Mrs. Cammie Henry died a few years later, in 1948.

I didn't sign my pictures at first, but after a year I put a C.H. I never did learn to write in any language, but I made the C.H. by myself. Made it that way clean up until I saw that they was too many C.H.'s around here. You know who I'm talking about—little Cammie Henry was so *mean* sometimes, I thought maybe she would mess me up.

So I turned my *C* around. Anyway, it looked like to me if I take that *C* business and turned it around the other way, it'd be more friendly and nicer.

Success

In 1955, when I was sixty-eight years old, some people showed my pictures. One show was at the Delgado Museum in New Orleans, Louisiana. Mine were the first paintings by a black person they ever had. I never been to New Orleans myself, never been any

"Saturday Night at the Honky-Tonk," 1963
 "So much noise at that honky-tonk down the road," Tebé once said, "that I used to couldn't sleep."

further than Baton Rouge. But I ain't interested. I don't travel, 'cause I know here and I don't know yonder.

The college in Natchitoches—that's on the highway, the navigating place above Melrose—showed some paintings, too. The college wouldn't let me in to see them at the same time as white folks. A white friend sneaked me in when wasn't nobody else around. I laughed when I saw some of them old pictures. "Where did you get that one?" I said. "I don't remember that one!"

That same year, François come and got me one night. Said he was cleaning out old furniture and tools from the African House. He wanted me to paint pictures to put in there. He bought them big old boards, and I painted the African House pictures in my house. Took about a month.

I painted a map of Cane River, a wedding, revival, cotton picking, pecan harvest, juke place, wake, funeral, and baptizing. Same kind like I been making for a while. I like to paint the same pictures over and over, but every one is a little different. Sure is.

In 1962, Mr. Pipes brought me some boards with pieces of colored paper on them. Asked me to look at them and make a new kind of painting.

Here's one—I don't know myself what that is. I just made that up, you know. I was sitting down painting and studying about different things, and I don't know how come I made all that. I bet I couldn't make that no more. It done something to my head. But it's pretty, though.

I made over a hundred of them new kind of paintings. Did them with a brush, not my fingers. You know, if you think about doing something, you can do it with a brush easy. And it be different. You got to have patience to paint, yes, you do.

I gave up making these paintings after a year 'cause they make my head sweat. But I like them myself. I wish I had them now.

They was lots more shows in the 1970s. Way off in New York and California. Now so many folks want me to make them some pictures. Rich folks from Paris, Mexico, South America, Ireland. I got more work than I can ever get through.

"Flower Garden," circa 1963. Tebé painted this abstract after seeing patterns in magazine advertisements.

Tebé in 1945, around the age of fifty-nine

See all those boards there? People bring me boards from all over the state. Some of them tell me they got lost trying to find this here place. Some of them mail the boards to me. My daughter Mary, she read what is written in the letters and on the backs of those things—names and addresses. Them people keep calling me by long distance and asking, am I through? Through! I ain't even started. I don't know when I'll ever get them done.

People ask for certain background colors, like red. Aw, shoot! Some people are too botheration! Hard to suit. You got to put the paint to match that what's already in the picture. The background changes, that's the kind of paint I have, and half the time I ain't never got the same color.

After a while I started getting fifty cents for a painting, then a dollar, then ten, and now it's up to one fifty. Painting's been a gift from God. It's helped me buy an electric icebox, stove, freezer, radio, television, and a bathroom.

And I have a secondhand car. Well, you know how it is, when you get as old as I am and living so far from town, you have to have a car in case you got to get to a doctor in a hurry. But the doctor say I am going to live a long time.

Moving

"Quilt," *1938*
The big Melrose house is in the middle, Ghana House is on the left, and African House is on the right.

Sometimes I just know things. I don't exactly know how I know them, but I know them. I can tell if company's coming, even on a stormy night when nobody's out on the road. If a letter comes and there's something in it for me, I know it.

I know about voodoo beads. One time I give François a quilt backed with paper. He hung that up 'cause it was light, you know. The wind was blowing it, so I laid two strings of buttons over the quilt. "Them voodoo beads," I told him, "they'll keep anything from hurting it."

And I know that what they did to François wasn't right. He stayed on at Melrose until 1970, when the Henrys moved him out. I don't know how come. Well, I guess they didn't have nobody to cook for him anymore. He didn't want to leave from there. He could die right there.

I had painted a heap of pictures for him, and they took his pictures! They sure took them. All them Henrys—Sister, too. Took them or sold them at auction. Those things were his'n. They done wrong, but they paying for it. When God put you down on your bed a long time, you paying for something wrong you done done.

That Sister, she something else. I know her from like that—I know! She don't like none of us people. Don't like none of her brothers, or nobody, or nothing!

"It's Tour Time," circa 1975
Creole women give daily tours of Melrose, which was named a National Historic Landmark in 1974.

Tebé's cabin after it was remodeled.

After I left Melrose in 1978, they moved my old cabin near the big house. Over on the field side by the spillway. They got it cleaned up pretty good. Put in plumbing and electricity. Made it a Baptist Sunday School house. Emmanuel died in that house, you know.

I bought a trailer up the road from Melrose. Next to my daughter Mary, her son Frank, and his daughter Quida. So I keep painting 'cause I got to help them out. And there's the two-hundred-dollar trailer payment to meet every month. I got behind on my car one time and I swear to God, I like to took a fit. My children say, "Oh, Mama, you don't got to worry," but shoot, I worry. I'm not like them.

Sometime I don't have a nickel to get my gas. Got to wait, you know, until I make it, and then pay. If I borrow something from somebody, I just hate it if I can't pay them right aways. Maybe someday I go borrow something and that the very time I can't paint nothing. Then what am I going to sell? Can't sell one unless I paint it, and that's what I worry about.

40

Still Working

Tebé's colorful quilt top resembles story banners from Benin, West Africa.

So I still paint a little. Quilt some, too. I made this quilt. Pieced it up myself, but I can't piece no more. I made that quilt year before last. You think that's pretty? It's real clean. Because I might get sick and I don't like nothing dirty what I'm going to sleep on! I had about six of them quilts, and I covered up with them when it was cold last year. I couldn't come out from under them things!

I sure felt like a dog today. Don't know what a dog feels, but I be feeling like one. Maybe you right. I worked too hard in my lifetime. Some people say work will kill you. Some of these so-called workers today would keel right over and die if they had to dog it as hard as I once had to.

All I know is, I do the best I can. When I was picking cotton for Cammie Henry, raising my family, and painting my pictures, I do what the Lord seem to tell me to do, and not worry my mind about things I can't do a thing about.

Visitors, now, I can do something about them. François can't come 'cause he's blind and can't get out much. Calls every day, though. Cammie Junior calls, too. Mildred Bailey from the college comes down every week or so. She a doctor or something. Whatever, me, I likes her. She sits and talks, just like home folks. And when old-timers come, I like to speak French with them.

But if people I don't know stop by, I tell them, "Clementine Hunter? She lives just

François Mignon once called his friend "Clementine the Mysterious."

on down the road a piece." Some pure-dee hillbillies came by one time. All the mens and ladies barefeeted. Wouldn't let them have any pictures no how! I don't even keep my pictures here now. Don't want anybody hunting them. I don't want to start them strangers here.

Yeah, I know they sold one of my paintings a few years back for $2,500. They *ought* to be valuable. They takes a lot of trouble! Specially for a ninety-year-old. I still chop my own wood, you know. Keep a garden, too.

Well, I got to put Tiny to bed in the other room. I shut him up in there 'cause I'm scared he'll be running all about here in the night. He'll call me to open the door in the morning. Tiny ain't got no fleas 'cause he stay inside.

What time do I go to sleep? Well, sometimes I'll sit up here in this chair until eleven o'clock if I don't have no company or nothing. Sometimes I'll just sit there and drop off to sleep, then wake up and say my prayers and go to bed. Get up about eight.

I don't paint at night no more. I can paint just as good at night, but I stopped when I moved here to the trailer—don't know why. I got my small room in the back set up for painting.

It's my bedroom, too, but I don't sleep there 'cause somebody might come in and go all the way back there. Well, I don't be scared, but I wasn't so brave when I first moved here, 'cause I wasn't used to it.

My eyes ain't as good as they used to be, but they still good yet. Sometimes when I paint in the sun and it's warm and it kind of hurts my eyes, then I wear glasses. Hearing, same thing. I can still hear. Some people can't hear nothing! Sometimes I get in my mind to quit painting, 'cause I got sinus in my head and arthritis in my hands. But then another picture comes in my mind.

People say when I go, my ghost will haunt Cane River. That's what they say. When I go, I don't want to come back. I want to go to heaven. I'll leave all my pictures. Lord, there are enough of them. If you laid all my paintings out, they would reach from here to Lord knows where.

Now, this here yellow paint—it's kind of like I been using, but it ain't yellow enough. And the green is just too dark, just too dark. A bird wouldn't nest in a tree that dark. So when you go into town, would you bring me back some paint? I sure do thank you.

Afterword

Tebé's doctor was right when he said she would live a long time. Though her pace slowed when she was in her late nineties, she never gave up painting. To meet the demand for her art, she painted thousands of watermelons, zinnias, and redbirds on key chains, gourds, and plastic milk jugs.

Making art was a comfort to her. Most important, the income helped her remain independent for the rest of her life. Shortly before Thanksgiving 1987, Tebé painted her last bouquet of zinnias. She was bedridden at home for the next five weeks. On December 27, she entered Natchitoches Parish Hospital because of dehydration.

Anxious collectors rushed to her bedside so she could initial their early unsigned paintings. The artist died on January 1, 1988, around the age of 101. She had outlived everyone in her immediate family except one sister and one daughter.

Tebé holds a special place in art history. With the help of James "Mr. Pipes" Register, she won a fellowship from the Rosenwald Fund in 1945. Julian Rosenwald was a patron of the arts who funded six hundred African-American artists for their "worthy artistic endeavor." Tebé was the only self-taught artist to receive this honor.

She was also the first self-taught African-American woman artist to receive national media attention. *Look* featured her life and art in 1953. In 1956, Edward Steichen, a famous photographer, praised Tebé's innocent art in an article for *Holiday*. In 1979 the director of the Museum of American Folk Art called her "perhaps the most celebrated of all Southern contemporary painters." Between 1945 and 1987, more than fifty museums and galleries showed her works.

Since her death, Tebé's pictures have become more popular than ever. They are on permanent display at twenty-two museums around the country, and art galleries sell her small paintings for $1,000 to $4,000 each. Early paintings, abstracts, and larger paintings are priced at $10,000 each. The window-shade painting she made for

François Mignon recently sold for $60,000.

The rise in prices shows a growing appreciation of self-taught art, also called primitive, folk, or outsider art. Supporters say it is more genuine and honest than fine art, and many believe both are of equal importance. "Self-taught art is not bad fine art," claims one fan. "This art is all about the artist's life."

Self-taught art is similar to some twentieth-century fine art. Two modern American artists, William

Tebé's burial vault next to St. Augustine's Catholic Church, near the banks of Cane River

Johnson and Romare Bearden, studied European painting in Paris, France, but they later developed the folklike style that came naturally to Tebé. Using flat images and bright colors, Johnson and Bearden recorded African American history in their works. Johnson painted riverside baptisms, churchgoers, dancing couples, and sharecroppers from his native South Carolina. Bearden made paper collages of cabins and vegetable gardens that he remembered from his childhood in North Carolina.

These educated painters were in fine company, for Tebé was a painter of southern history, too. Unlike them, she worked at night after she had done her cooking, gardening, cleaning, and child-rearing. For thirty years, her only studio was a weathered cabin, her only light a kerosene lamp. She used her lap as an easel, a scrap of plywood for a palette, and a cedar shingle or paper bag as a canvas.

Tebé never kept any of her paintings. "I see a picture in my mind," she once said. "Then I put it down, and then I'm finished with it."

Though she left no paintings to her descendants, she gave them the gift of history.

"Gourds," circa 1950
In Tebé's time, workers dried the gourds and split them to make drinking cups.

Young Diana Davis, Tebé's great-granddaughter, understood her legacy well. She read these words at Tebé's funeral: "Great-Grandmother Clementine, we know times were hard, for you have told us so. You showed it in your paintings so the world would know."

Sources

Books

Bearden, Romare, and Harry Henderson. *A History of African-American Artists from 1792 to the Present.* New York: Pantheon, 1993.

Mignon, François, and Clementine Hunter. *Melrose Plantation Cookbook.* Natchitoches, La.: [François Mignon], 1956.

Rosenak, Chuck, and Jan Rosenak. *Museum of American Folk Art Encyclopedia of Twentieth-Century American Folk Art and Artists.* New York: Abbeville Press, 1990.

Turner, Lorenzo Dow. *Africanisms in the Gullah Dialect.* Chicago: University of Chicago Press, 1949.

Wilson, James L. *Clementine Hunter: American Folk Artist.* Gretna, La: Pelican, 1988.

Periodicals

Jones, Anne Hudson. "The Centennial of Clementine Hunter." *Women's Art Journal,* Spring/Summer 1987, 23–27.

Lamothe, Eva. "A Visit with Clementine Hunter: Painter of Visions and Dreams." *Arts Quarterly,* New Orleans Museum of Art, April-May-June 1985, 32–34.

Miller, Herschel. "Clementine Hunter—American Primitive." *New Orleans,* December 1968, 6–11.

Morris, Steven. "The Primitive Art of Clementine Hunter." *Ebony,* May 1969, vol. 24, 144–48.

Ryan, Robert, and Yvonne Ryan. "Clementine Hunter: A New Orleans Salute." *Arts Quarterly,* New Orleans Museum of Art, January February-March 1985, 14–15.

Willard, Charlotte. "Innocence Regained." *Look,* June 16, 1963, vol. 17, 102–105.

Newspapers

Bounds, Mary C. "Art With Heart." *The Dallas Morning News,* September 9, 1982, sec. A, 1–2.

King, Elaine. "Clementine Hunter, Artist, Found on a Talkative Day." *The Shreveport [Louisiana] Times,* February 2, 1975, sec. C, 4.

McDonald, Margaret. "Clementine the Painter." *The Shreveport [Louisiana] Times,* May 8, 1955, sec. F, 2.

Northrop, Guy. "Clementine Hunter: First Look For Memphis." *The [Memphis] Appeal,* May 23, 1976, "Fanfare Magazine," 10.

Additional resources include *Women of Cane River*, Natchitoches, La.: Northwestern State University of Louisiana, 1980 (distributed by the Center for the Study of Southern Culture, University of Mississippi); interview tapes 1–22 and letters, programs, and clippings from scrapbooks 2–3 and 28–30 in the Mildred Hart Bailey Collection, Archives and Special Collections, Cammie G. Henry Research Center, Eugene P. Watson Memorial Library, Northwestern State University of Louisiana, Natchitoches.

Photo Credits

Pages 9, 16, 32–33, 37, 42: Courtesy of Archives and Special Collections, Cammie G. Henry Research Center, Eugene P. Watson Memorial Library, Northwestern State University of Louisiana, Natchitoches

Pages 18, 22, 24, 34, 38: Mildred Hart Bailey Collection

Pages 10, 15, 17, 25–29, 41, 46, front cover: Courtesy of Jack and Ann Brittain and Children

Pages 2, 12–13, 20–21, 23, 31, 36, 39, back cover: Thomas N. Whitehead Collection

Pages 14, 40, 45: Courtesy of Mary E. Lyons

Page 30: Courtesy of Curtis Guillet

Acknowledgments

The following people generously answered questions or directed me to other sources:
Ann Brittain, Robert Cargo, Shelby Gilley, Curtis Guillet, John Ridley, Judy Saslow, Pati Threatt, Sandra Tradero, and Marcia Weber. Special thanks to my researcher, Kelly Tetterton.

APR 1 3 1998